MW00811131

Advance Praise for
Millennials' Guide to Real Estate

"Ever wished that school taught you about real estate? Well, problem solved! *Millennials' Guide to Real Estate* is insightful and to the point. Zach Brickner is one of the best real estate professionals around, and this book serves as a download of his many years of experience. Instead of guessing what to search on the Internet and hoping you get good advice, pick this book up and let it guide you to the start of your real estate empire."
-Reggie D. Ford, entrepreneur and bestselling author of *Perseverance Through Severe Dysfunction: Breaking the Curse of Intergenerational Trauma as a Black Man in America.*

"As a licensed real estate salesperson in New York City, *Millennials' Guide to Real Estate* is a great overview for clients buying their first home. It covers everything buyers need to know. What a great resource!"
-Shimaa Anwar, Licensed Real Estate Salesperson, Top Producer & Team Leader, The Anwar Team at LG Fairmont, New York

"Real estate transactions have changed over the course of every generation; however, *Millennials' Guide to Real Estate* explains the current landscape in an easy and concise manner. I recommend this book to anyone looking to buy, sell, or become a real estate agent today or in the future."
-Hunter Connelly, CEO of Parks / Village / Pilkerton

MILLENNIALS'
GUIDE TO
REAL ESTATE

What No One Ever Told You About
Investing in Your Future

WINDING PATHWAY BOOKS

Zachary Brickner

Jennifer P. Wisdom

Published by Winding Pathway Books

WINDING PATHWAY BOOKS

ISBN (print): 978-1-954374-08-9
ISBN (e-book): 978-1-954374-06-5
Book design by: Wendy C. Garfinkle
Cover design by Jada Fontanez
Photo credit: Diego G. Diaz

For more information or bulk orders, visit: millennialsguides.com

Printed in the United States of America

Foreword

Millennial: A person reaching young adulthood in the early 21st century.

When Parks Realty started in 1975, millennial was a thousand years, not a generation. As we have experienced the changes in generations (Generation X, Xennials, Generation Y, etc.), one thing that has remained a constant is the dream of home ownership. One of the greatest challenges and joys in my life has been working in the real estate industry and providing mentorship, leadership, and sharing my passion for real estate with all those who are part of the Parks Realty family.

It has been one of my greatest joys to see the progress Zach Brickner has made during his time with Parks. Zach joined our firm as a real estate agent more than 3 years ago as an experienced agent in the Nashville market. His maturity, knowledge of the local market, and his customer service is unparalleled. When the decision came for a new managing broker for our office in West Nashville, the decision was easy. The entire management team's first thought was Zach Brickner.

Graduating college, your first job, marriage, buying your first home are all life events that mark milestones in our lives. While we all may have some idea of how to hit those goals, the purchase of your home is for most of us the largest financial investment of our lives. While the process of finding your home has changed over the last 45 years, having a trusted advisor for the process is still key to a successful and stress-free process.

As a Millennial, Zach brings a unique perspective to this process. Not only does he work in the real estate industry, but he has also purchased and sold his personal homes. Technology, lending, interest rates all are changing in real estate, but what does not change is having someone like Zach walk alongside you and provide the guidance to help you find your dream home.

Zach, I am so proud of you and your successes. I'm thankful that you are a part of what we have built together at Parks and know that you will continue to have great successes in your career and that your guide to real estate will be a tremendous success.

- Bob Parks, Chairman of Parks/Village/Pilkerton

Contents

Foreword 7

INTRODUCTION 1

HOW TO USE THIS BOOK 3

Part I. Real Estate Basics 5

Chapter 1: What Does it Mean to Invest in Real Estate? 7

Chapter 2: What is the Difference Between Buying and Renting? ... 9

Chapter 3: What is the Process for Buying a Home? 11

Chapter 4: How Do I Know it's Time to Purchase a Home? 15

Chapter 5: Real Estate Agents and How They Operate 19

Chapter 6: What is the Difference Between Banks and Mortgage
Companies? 23

Chapter 7: How and When to Get Pre-Approved 25

Chapter 8: How to Find the Most Up-To-Date and Accurate Listings
.... 27

Chapter 9: What are Closing Expenses and How Do They Affect My
Purchase? 29

Part II. Buying Real Estate 31

Chapter 10: Where to Start When Preparing to Buy a Home 33

Chapter 11: Potential Pitfalls of Purchasing a Home 35

Chapter 12: How to Pick the Best Real Estate Agent for You 37

Chapter 13: Kinds of Properties You Might Want to Consider 39

Chapter 14: Types of Home Loans 43

Chapter 15: Location, Location, Location! 47

Chapter 16: Showings! Time to Go See Some Homes 49

Chapter 17: Negotiating From the Buyer's Perspective 51

Chapter 18: What to Know During the Inspection Phase 53

Chapter 19: When to Walk Away From a Contract 57

Chapter 20: Do's and Don'ts of Closing Week 59

Part III. Settling Into Your New Home 61

Chapter 21: Common Move-In Issues 63

Chapter 22: Renovations: Are They Worth It? 67

Chapter 23: Renting Out Your Home 69

Part IV. Selling Real Estate 71

    Chapter 24: Steps in Selling a Home 73

    Chapter 25: Where to Start When Preparing to Sell a Home 77

    Chapter 26: Potential Pitfalls When Selling a Home 79

    Chapter 27: Working with a Real Estate Agent When Selling Your
        Home 81

    Chapter 28: What are Foreclosures and Short Sales? 83

    Chapter 29: Marketing 101 85

    Chapter 30: How to Show Your Home 87

    Chapter 31: Negotiating From the Seller's Perspective 89

    Chapter 32: The Final Steps of Selling: To the Closing Table and
        Beyond 91

Part V. Being a Real Estate Agent 93

    Chapter 33: Should I Become a Real Estate Agent? 95

    Chapter 34: What Does Being a Real Estate Agent Involve? 97

    Chapter 35: What is Required to Become a Real Estate Agent? 99

    Chapter 36: Nine Keys to Success When Working in Real Estate . 101

Glossary 105

For Further Reading 111

Acknowledgements 113

About the Authors 115

Additional Books by the Authors 117

INTRODUCTION

I wanted to start off by saying thank you. Thank you for investing in yourself and your future by picking up this book. Real estate can often seem like a scary endeavor. It is one of those things like taxes or check-writing that you expect school to teach you at some level of education. It's an expectation that, unless you search out information on real estate, often goes unfulfilled. It feels like I spent an entire year learning about the Pythagorean Theorem, but that information was never helpful to me. I hear and talk about real estate daily, but I had to teach myself the ins and outs. Either way, I am happy that you are here to learn more and, hopefully, be better equipped to buy, sell, renovate, and invest with the best of them.

Honestly, I just want Millennials to have the same opportunities at relatively the same cost as the generations before us. Is that too much to ask for? While I do love avocado toast, it seems silly to think that I can't buy into real estate because of a couple of wild brunch purchases. It feels that way sometimes, right? Many publications and articles blame Millennials for this and that and say it's the "reason" why things are harder for us. Well, I don't believe that. I believe we were dealt a difficult hand as a generation. We had the most significant recession of our lives right as we entered the job market in 2008. We had the first pandemic in 100 years right as we were entering our peak earning years. We Millennials haven't had it easy, so I am hopeful I can help you find success and financial stability through real estate.

While real estate can seem scary, it is one of the most stable buy-and-hold investments that a person can make in their lifetime. You have probably seen the statistic that goes something like "90% of millionaires are invested in real estate." Not only does real estate typically appreciate over an extended time horizon, but it also can become an asset that pays *you* over time. All of these things add up to an investment that is safe and lucrative. I hope you will read this book and be confident enough to get into the real estate market sooner rather than later and position yourself for a happy and wealthy future.

Lastly, I want to talk about real estate as a career. Becoming a real estate agent has been one of the best decisions I have ever made. Although it has taken a lot of hard work, it has provided a fantastic life with a lot of flexibility. If you ever decide to get into real estate as an agent, remember these main things:

1. Success takes time. Although it seems like it happens overnight for some people, I promise they have put in the work. Put in the work and good things will come.
2. Show up. Show up to sales meetings. Show up to networking mixers. Show up to family gatherings. Show up when your friends get together. You cannot win if you do not show up.
3. Do what you say you are going to do. No one will fault you for not being able to do something, but if you commit ahead of time, you need to do it. People will not want to work with you if they can't trust your word.

I hope you enjoy this book and I hope you learn something you didn't know before. Please feel free to connect with me on my social media pages:

Instagram: @z_bricksquad
Facebook: www.facebook.com/zacharybrickner
LinkedIn: www.linkedin.com/in/zachary-brickner-8a140b51/
Tiktok: (I'm joking...I am only on Tiktok to watch videos)

Zachary Brickner

HOW TO USE THIS BOOK

You've got questions about real estate; we have answers! There's no need to read this book from cover to cover in order. Instead, we suggest you look through the contents, find your question, and read about it. Start with whatever is interesting to you, what you're curious about, or what worries you.

We recommend being patient, curious and mindful. Then show up.

Be patient. Remember that it can take a long time for a solution to work out. Just like how therapy or exercise can take months or years to get the results you want, same goes for purchasing property. This is where having goals and support systems can come in handy. They will remind you of where you are headed. Of course, if you feel like you aren't making any progress, it's valid to try something new, but sometimes the best thing is to keep at the grind.

Be curious. Be open to new experiences, new people, new perspectives. That is how you end up with your dream home. Most new ideas are a load of rubbish, but occasionally, you'll find something new, wonderful, and exciting where you didn't expect it.

Be mindful. Keep in mind what you care about and what you want to accomplish. Where you live and how you invest your money is not a single problem with a single solution. Rather, it's about constantly asking "Does this work for me and for others?"

In addition to reading this book, take steps to move forward. When you're not sure about what to do, this book will be here for you. After you read and when you're ready, it's time to get up and get things done!

Part I. Real Estate Basics

This section answers some important questions about how to get started with buying real estate and who the main players are, including the buyer, seller, real estate agent, and lender. Note we refer to "homes" to mean a home, an apartment, or any other place you'd like to buy.

Chapter 1: What Does it Mean to Invest in Real Estate?

At its core, investing in real estate is simple. It is the act of purchasing real estate to live in, rent out, flip, or develop, and then reaping the fruits of the labor. Of course, in real life it feels more complicated. In this chapter, we will discuss each of these scenarios and how it works.

1. **Investing in real estate that you live in as your home is the simplest version of investment.** The buyer of a property makes a purchase and pays down what they owe on the asset. During this time, the owner can be increasing the value of the property through appreciation (appreciation is the natural growth of the value of property over time) or smart renovations that increase the value of the property. These investments are unrealized (meaning the owner doesn't get money in their pocket) until the owner sells or rents the property.

2. **Investing in rental properties is a slightly different animal.** When a buyer purchases a rental property, they make money through the exact same venues as living in the property except they can also potentially have a positive cash flow. Positive cash flow is when your incoming profits from rent are higher than the outgoing costs of the loan, insurance, maintenance, and taxes.

3. **Flipping real estate is probably the riskiest type of real estate investment.** When someone "flips" a home, they buy a home that is in slightly worse shape and then make the necessary repairs to increase the value. Usually this is done with houses, but it's possible to flip condos or co-ops. Flipping looks glamorous on television shows, but it's quite risky. In a good scenario, the home's value increases more than the cost of those repairs and the buyer makes a profit. There are

situations where the buyer does not make a profit, such as when they spend too much on the renovation. Additionally, they could over-estimate the demand in the market and have the home sit without selling (while the seller must keep paying the mortgage). Again, flipping homes has the highest risk.

4. **Real estate development** is the type of investing that has the highest barrier to entry. In most development scenarios, an investor needs a lot of money or assets to effectively get started. Different examples of development are building a condominium, subdividing lots to build multiple residences, or purchasing an apartment building with multiple tenants. Making a profit from these include selling units that are built, collecting rents from tenants, or general appreciation of land.

5. **Where do I start?** Your options for real estate likely depend on how much capital (money to invest) you have, how much debt you have, or how stable of a job you have. It could be one of these factors or it could be all three.

See Also:

Chapter 8: How to Find the Most Up-To-Date and Accurate
        Listings
Chapter 11: Potential Pitfalls of Purchasing a Home
Chapter 19: When to Walk Away from a Contract

Chapter 2: What is the Difference Between Buying and Renting?

How do you know whether to buy or rent? When a person is renting, they don't own the property, and they are paying rent to someone who does own the property. Simple as that, right? Actually, it is much deeper than that and a couple of factors come into play that can influence your decisions. Let's look at the pros and cons of renting and buying:

1. **Renting has pros and cons.** In favor of renting, there is a lower upfront cost, flexibility to move and not incur broker costs, fewer maintenance costs, no property taxes to pay, and relatively low commitment because you can leave once your lease is up. On the other hand, renting tenants are effectively paying the bills of the owner, they have little to no ownership of the space, and the money being spent is not being invested in any way. Some people call paying rent "lighting money on fire" because it is gone forever. Others relish not being responsible for maintenance and being free to leave with relatively little hassle. While renting comes with a much lower commitment threshold, it is undoubtedly not a good financial plan long term – unless rent is very low, and you don't want the responsibility of managing a property.

2. **Purchasing a home,** on the other hand, can be a fiscally responsible decision for long term wealth. Home purchasers have true ownership, a long-term investment, real estate appreciation (which means your investment usually gains value over time), asset acquisition, and pathways towards future income streams (such as renting it out to tenants.) Purchasing, however, also includes high up-front costs, property taxes, maintenance costs, and less flexibility.

3. **There are several buy vs. rent calculators available online.** These calculators factor in your current rent; likely purchase

cost of a home; additional ongoing costs for utilities, taxes, etc.; and how long you plan to stay in the property to see what is financially better for you over time. See the For Further Reading section for links to these calculators.

4. A home --whether house, apartment, or co-op -- will most likely be the biggest purchase that someone will ever make. That said, the first purchase is the hardest; however, every additional one gets easier and the inherent value gets compounded.

See Also:
Chapter 5: Real Estate Agents and How They Operate
Chapter 13: Kinds of Properties You Might Want to Consider
Chapter 21: Common Move-In Issues

Chapter 3: What is the Process for Buying a Home?

There are many steps in buying a home. Here's an overview of the main parts of the process.

1. **What do you want?** – The first step to finding a home is figuring out what type of property you want. How many bedrooms do you need? Do you need a garage or yard? Are you concerned about high levels of maintenance? Do you want to be close or far away from family and friends? Are you comfortable with renovating? All of these are questions you should answer when starting the real estate journey.

2. **Pre-approval/What can you afford?** – While you are looking at homes and figuring out what you want, you should know what you can afford. There are plenty of "mortgage calculators" online that make it easy to have an estimated monthly payment. This isn't a bad place to start; however, you will need to talk to a lender who is going to loan you the money. The lender will do a review of your finances to figure out exactly what price point you can search in.

3. **Find an agent.** While real estate agents aren't required, they definitely make the home buying process easier. From finding "coming soon" listings or negotiating the best price and terms, a great real estate agent can make the process smooth and fun! You can ask for referrals from friends or family or you can look for online reviews. Both of these options are solid for looking for a real estate agent.

4. **Look for homes.** Back in the day, only real estate agents had access to all of the listings. Today, listings are online in one place or another. It's a smart idea to send your real estate agent any listings online that you like. Make sure to only send

listings that you can afford. No one wants to waste time on homes you can't afford!

5. **Negotiate a contract.** Once you have found the home of your dreams, you – with the agent's help - are going to negotiate a contract to purchase the property. This is the first time you will negotiate the terms of the purchase until the inspection period (if applicable). Make sure to tell your agent all the items (furniture, appliances, etc.) you want to remain in the property as a part of the contract.

6. **Inspection.** Often, you will end up getting an inspection on the property. This is a data gathering period for you to assess all the potential risk in the property before moving forward with the purchase. You will often have a contingency that allows you to back out if the inspection comes back poorly. If you want to proceed, you will negotiate again over what (if anything) must be repaired before closing.

7. **Lots of paperwork.** There is a lot of paperwork within a real estate purchase. There is an agreement for sale between the buyer and seller, documents from the lender regarding the mortgage, and the real estate agent will have company-required documents that need signing. You will have time to review all documents and ask questions. Thankfully, most, if not all, of those documents can be e-signed so you can do it from your email.

8. **Closing.** Closing day is one of the happiest days! This is the day that you will go from being under contract to closed, and will officially own your piece of real estate. This is where the lender and real estate attorney will need the buyer to sign a plethora of documents. As always, make sure to ask questions when you are unsure. Once you have signed on the dotted lines, it's hard to go back!

9. **Move in.** Unless previously negotiated, once you close, the property will be yours and you can move in! Depending on

your timeline, it is probably smart to schedule the movers sooner rather than later. Good moving companies will be in high demand, so you want to schedule them before closing occurs.

See Also:
Chapter 16: Showings! Time to Go See Some Homes
Chapter 10: Where to Start When Preparing to Buy a Home
Chapter 28: What are Foreclosures and Short Sales?

Chapter 4: How Do I Know it's Time to Purchase a Home?

Buying real estate is probably the biggest purchase most people will make in their lives. Many mortgages also come with a 30-year timeline (which can typically be paid off faster), so making a home purchase can appear incredibly daunting. It is a lot to take on, but the long-term benefits can be incredibly worthwhile. Here are a couple of questions that any purchaser should ask themselves.

1. **Is it a buyer's or seller's market?** A buyer's market is one where there is less demand for housing or obtaining a loan is easier, and, therefore, it is more beneficial for a buyer to purchase a home. Less demand generally means there are more homes to pick from. A buyer can see more home and get closer to exactly what they are looking for. Additionally, sellers are willing to give up more in negotiations because they are trying to court a potential buyer. On the other hand, when obtaining a loan is easier, it means that buying a home is cheaper due to lower than usual interest rates. A seller's market means that sellers can make more of their own demands with regards to how, when, and for how much they decide to sell their home. In a seller's market, a seller can negotiate a higher sales price, a better closing timeline, or even the removal of vital contingencies that are meant to protect a buyer. The seller has something that a buyer wants and since the buyer has less options, the buyer can be at the whim of a seller's desires.

2. **Have I talked to a lender, and do I have enough money to close?** The minimum down payment for a home is usually 3.5% of the purchase price (unless you are a veteran where it can go as low as 0% down). The closing costs of a purchase are typically going to be about 3% of the price of the home. With a $200,000 home as an example, in most cases a buyer will need between $12,000 and $15,000 (~6.5% of the

purchase price) of readily available cash to close. Please note these estimates are the minimum. Having more cash will give you more options. A couple of caveats: A buyer, in some markets, can negotiate that the seller pay some (or all) of their closing costs. Additionally, buyers will also need approximately $500 for a home inspection and more for other costs that may come up.

3. **What kind of credit score do I have?** A good credit score will directly affect the interest rate of the loan and therefore the purchasing power of the buyer. Good credit scores are generally above 650 or 700. You can get free credit reports from the three major credit reporting agencies; see the For Further Reading section. If you have missed a few utility or credit card payments that affected your credit, speak to a lender about how to improve those numbers. A good credit score when obtaining a loan will have a massive effect on how much money is paid out long term, and the life of the mortgage.

4. **Am I (or we, if you are considering purchasing with a partner) financially stable?** Financially stable means something different for every buyer; however, to purchase a home, buyers will need to be able to document their income and expense monthly and over the past few years. You shouldn't purchase a home if you don't know where your next paycheck is coming from.

5. **Is the kind of home you could afford something you want?** Online mortgage calculators can help you understand what a minimum monthly payment would be on a home (not including taxes, maintenance, or utilities). When you identify what you could afford, are homes at that price in a place where you want to live? What are the taxes like in this area? What would your work commute be like? Are there amenities nearby important to you, such as schools for children or nightlife?

6. **What if I'm not sure how to answer these questions?** It's okay if you don't know the answers to all of these. It's a process to buy a home, and many of these issues will be discussed in more depth in this book. Keep reading!

See Also:
Chapter 12: How to Pick the Best Real Estate Agent for You
Chapter 14: Types of Home Loans
Chapter 17: Negotiating From the Buyer's Perspective

Chapter 5: Real Estate Agents and How They Operate

In most situations, a buyer will need to commit to a real estate agent. Why should you work with a real estate agent, and what do they do?

1. **Real estate agents will have up-to-date access to all new listings in the area immediately.** Back in the day before I (ZB) was a real estate agent, a buyer would employ a real estate agent because only the agent had access to all the sales listings. This is no longer the case. You can search the Internet for listings, but real estate agents represent you and can assist you in the complexities of viewing homes, making an offer, getting an inspection, gaining access to lenders, and negotiating the final sale.

2. **Real estate agents know real estate.** They can listen to what you're interested in, and help you find the perfect property. They can share information about neighborhoods and the market and lots of other areas. They can also set up automatic alerts when new listings hit the market that meet the client's parameters. When homes become available, the agent also can help schedule appointments to see homes and help buyers evaluate each home they review.

3. **Hiring a real estate agent typically costs the buyer nothing.** We currently live in the era of cooperating commissions, which means the seller is often offering commission to a buyer's agent to bring a buyer to the property. While there can be brokerage or transaction fees, these are very small charges compared to the typical $1,000+ that commission brings in. Just think - if a licensed lawyer or doctor were free, how often would a person opt out of using their services?

4. **Real estate agents have expertise and work relationships they have built throughout their career that can benefit you.** Chances are your agent has worked with a lot of good real estate agents and managed a lot of sales, which means they can see red flags before a transaction gets derailed. Don't forget that a buyer will probably need an electrician, flooring company, roofer, contractor, or plumber at some point during the time they own their home. Good real estate agents have access to all these resources.

5. **Successful real estate agents do this every single day of their life.** Good ones are experts at their craft and know how to navigate transactions. Real estate agents are experts at negotiation and pointing out pitfalls, so a buyer is fully prepared for all situations. Often, they will be able to communicate their way through the potential ups and downs of any contract. While not every pitfall can be avoided, a good real estate agent warns the buyer about its possibility and has the expertise to navigate through it without too much trouble.

6. **If one agent is great, then are more agents better?** It's possible to talk to many agents and theoretically have many agents working for you, but it is also a very fast way to burn bridges. Real estate is a business built around loyalty. And you don't want several agents calling the same sellers for home tours. For any purchase, you should generally work with only one agent.

7. **Once a buyer has picked the perfect agent and lender for the purchase, then it is all about looking for homes and submitting offers.** We cannot stress it enough how important it is to see multiple homes with the real estate agent. Some of the smoothest transactions have begun with agents and clients going to see a handful of properties together just to get to know each other and navigate how the process is going to

work. The better the relationship is with the real estate agent, typically, the smoother the transaction will be.

See Also:
Chapter 24: Steps in Selling a Home
Chapter 27: Working with a Real Estate Agent When Selling Your Home
Chapter 33: Should I Become a Real Estate Agent?

Chapter 6: What is the Difference Between Banks and Mortgage Companies?

Most people who buy properties finance the sale through a bank or mortgage company. Let's discuss how those are different entities and what that means for you.

1. **What do you mean by banks and mortgage companies?** Banks are organizations such as US Bank, Wells Fargo, Chase, or local credit unions that often offer many services, such as checking, savings, mortgages, and more. Mortgage companies are organizations such as Guaranteed Rate, Steadfast Mortgage, First Community Mortgage, etc. that have a primary business of mortgages.

2. **Can you help me understand the difference between banks and mortgage companies?** I (ZB) like to use the analogy of buying light bulbs as an example. Any hardware store can sell a lightbulb but it's universally accepted that a lightbulb store is going to have the most options that fit a client's needs. That is like the difference between a bank and a mortgage company. Any bank can do a mortgage, but it is a mortgage company's sole job and priority to do mortgages. Mortgage companies are inherently better and more flexible because of that.

3. **There's also ... the relationship.** It is imperative that at some level of relationship exists between either the buyer and the lender or the agent and the lender. Is having a checking account with a bank considered having a relationship? No. Is having investments with a bank considered having a relationship? Probably not. A personal relationship is where the lender completing the loan *cares* about the outcome of the transaction because of a professional affiliation.

4. **How do I choose between a bank or a mortgage company?** At the end of the day, banks are big entities with a handful of departments that also close loans. Mortgage companies are

businesses built entirely around closing home loans. It may not matter which one a buyer decides to go with; however, if a buyer has one bad transaction, they will never want it again.

See also:
Chapter 3: What is the Process for Buying a Home?
Chapter 7: When and How to Get Pre-Approved
Chapter 10: Types of Home Loans

Chapter 7: How and When to Get Pre-Approved

If you will be getting a loan to purchase (as opposed to paying cash for the full amount), the first step is to get pre-approved for a loan. How does one get pre-approved?

1. **The first step is to pick a lender.** The lender you choose will end up being your financial partner throughout this entire process. Lenders can have different rates, programs, or processes that can help or hinder the process. Often, a real estate agent will have preferred lenders they recommend. It's not a bad idea to explore these options first.

2. **A lender will seek to determine the buyer's debt to income profile.** A lender will weigh all the client's assets and income versus the amount of outstanding debt they have. The lender will request documents including tax returns, 1099s, pay stubs, details regarding assets (think cars, property, etc.), and verification of any debts. They may also ask you to complete a mortgage application. Remember: do not lie on these documents or to a lender. Mortgage fraud is a federal offense!

3. **Ideally buyers obtain pre-approval approximately 6 months before they want to buy a home.** In this scenario, they can financially get all their ducks in a row to make sure the purchase is as smooth as possible. Sometimes there are issues with how much debt a buyer has. Other times they need to improve their credit score to obtain a better interest rate. All these factors play into being approved to buy a home and a good lender will tell you how to improve them. Additionally, these factors will all affect the buying power of the purchaser, i.e., how expensive of a home a buyer can afford.

4. **The lender will provide a pre-approval letter.** This letter is the word of the lender/mortgage company that you can purchase a property at a certain price point. It also clarifies how much

the bank is willing to loan you – not including any down payment that you will be providing. Note this amount can possibly be adjusted, but it provides a general estimate of how much mortgage you can obtain.

5. **The Pre-Approval process is not the end.** First, it only lasts about 90 days. If you do not get a home closed within that time, the lender will need to run your credit again. When you do get under contract, you will still need to finish the entire loan with the lender. They will often request updates on bank statements and pay stubs from your employer.

6. **Once you are pre-approved, it's off to see homes!**

See Also:
Chapter 14: Types of Home Loans
Chapter 18: What to Know During the Inspection Phase
Chapter 19: When to Walk Away From a Contract

Chapter 8: How to Find the Most Up-To-Date and Accurate Listings

One thing that has changed rapidly since the invention of the internet is that real estate agents are not the keepers of the listings. Statistics say that more than 50% of buyers start looking at homes online more than 9 months out from their intended closing date. How can you check out the market before you jump in?

1. **A word of caution:** even though buyers can go online and effectively see about 95% of all the listings that are available for sale, some websites do not have up-to-date listings or just entirely incorrect listings. It's a wild shift in real estate that has many buyers asking what is real, incorrect, or just pulled out of thin air.

2. **Let's discuss the big dogs first.** Zillow (zillow.com) and Trulia (trulia.com) are wonderful resources. They have a plethora of information that is integral to the home searching process. With that having been said, they are not always accurate or up to date. Some companies (think Crye-Leike or Remax) with real estate agents and listing share their data with them, and some do not. Estimates of home worth can also vary wildly. This uncertainty can throw off a buyer with regards to the current housing inventory or even prices.

3. **The most accurate and current listings are at Realtor.com and the Multiple Listing Service (MLS).** A local MLS is the real estate agent's subscription service for housing listings; the MLSs usually have a customer-facing version as well that buyers can search. Realtor.com integrates listings from local MLSs to provide a comprehensive search engine for all available properties for sale. Typically speaking, Realtor.com and these local websites give the consumer plenty of information including if a home is under contract or not. That

way there isn't as much wasted time getting excited over a home that is no longer available!

4. **What do I look for online?** Does the home have photos yet? Are they professional photos or done with a camera phone? Does it look like the seller is hiding something? These are all things to look out for when looking online for listings. Lastly, it's worth reading the listing agent's comments on the listing if they are available. They will sometimes provide some helpful insight into the home.

See Also:
Chapter 11: Potential Pitfalls of Purchasing a Home
Chapter 15: Location! Location! Location!
Chapter 22: Renovations: Are They Worth It?

Chapter 9: What are Closing Expenses and How Do They Affect My Purchase?

Closing expenses, at their core, are costs and fees that a buyer or seller must pay to close a real estate transaction. These costs are in addition to a down payment on the home.

1. **What do closing costs include?** On a buyer's side of the transaction, closing expenses include but are not limited to transfer taxes, recording fees, attorney fees, title insurance, preparation of loan documents, credit report, premium required for private mortgages, hazard and flood insurance, required deposits for insurance premiums and taxes, prepaid loan interest, association fees, and any costs associated with obtaining and closing a loan. On most transactions, these expenses come out to around ~3% of the purchase price of the property.

2. **Who pays the buyer's closing costs?** A buyer always pays the down payment; the buyer and seller can negotiate over who pays closing costs. It is not typical that one side or the other covers these expenses – everything is negotiable. Buyers should plan to pay for these costs or negotiate that the seller covers part of them. Lastly, buyer's closing expenses are paid at closing. No worries here though – a good lender would have explained these in full during the pre-approval process.

3. **Who pays the seller's closing costs?** On a seller's side of a transaction, closing expenses include but are not limited to any loans or liens on the property, any outstanding association fees, attorney fees, wire or transfer fees associated with paying off debts, and real estate agent commissions, if applicable. These fees are much more difficult to predict and vary on a transaction-by-transaction basis. Also, these fees are taken out of the proceeds that the seller would receive from the sale of their property. If the seller is not making a profit on the sale,

they may have to bring those additional funds to the closing table to close the deal.

See Also:
Chapter 7: How and When to Get Pre-Approved
Chapter 17: Negotiating From the Buyer's Perspective
Chapter 20: Do's and Don'ts of Closing Week

Part II. Buying Real Estate

This section covers everything you need to know about buying real estate, including how to get started, pitfalls, choosing an agent to help you and much more!

Chapter 10: Where to Start When Preparing to Buy a Home

There are only a handful of items needed to buy a home that are entirely in the buyer's control; a good place to start is by getting those items under control. The phrase "worry about what one can control" comes to mind.

1. **The down payment.** More than likely, a buyer is going to need to bring at least 3.5% of the purchase price to the closing table to buy a home. This payment is a "good faith" amount towards the loan that the buyer is acquiring. While the 3.5% is a good market, a smart buyer will continue to save as much as possible so they will easily clear that threshold if possible. In some cases, you can use gifted funds as a down payment, but you will often have to document where the money came from. Lastly, you will need to provide some of this down payment at the time you sign a contract. This is called earnest or trust money. This is a "good faith" payment to the seller that you will stay in the contract legally.

2. **The buyer's debt and credit score.** Debt affects both a buyer's debt-to-income ratio and their credit score. A buyer should start paying off debts because it will directly affect their ability to obtain a mortgage. Some debts are better to pay off first (e.g., pay off credit cards first because they likely have the highest interest rates). You may want to consult with a lender to get advice on the order in which to pay off debt to maximize your credit score.

3. **Timeline.** It would be helpful to identify what your timeline is. If your lease is ending or if you are getting a new job in another area, those might be helpful guides to inform your timeline. Generally, lenders look for buyers applying for a mortgage to have had a job for at least 6 months, though that is flexible if a buyer has a strong work history. Most people

33

want to minimize the amount of overlap between purchase and rental (so you're not paying for both rent and mortgage at the same time), but some overlap can be helpful when you are moving. Figure out what kind of timeline might make sense for you.

4. **Interview and pick a real estate agent that you trust.** Remember that you are hiring this professional to give you sound advice but also counsel you through the entire process. If someone is erratic or not trustworthy, it's going to make the experience more difficult. Additionally, the best real estate agents have a process that will feel professional and clean.

5. **Figure out what you want in a home.** Buyers can educate themselves on certain neighborhoods and their price points. This way a buyer sets expectations with themselves about where they can live and for how much money. There is nothing worse than thinking a neighborhood is within reach and being constantly disappointed by the new listings located there.

See Also:
Chapter 2: What is the Difference Between Buying and Renting?
Chapter 3: What is the Process for Buying a Home?
Chapter 12: How to Pick the Best Real Estate Agent for You

Chapter 11: Potential Pitfalls of Purchasing a Home

Buying a home can be scary. There are plenty of issues that can arise during the process or after closing. The best thing a buyer can do is be prepared for problems that may arise and know how best to counteract them. Here are some of the most significant issues:

1. **During a contract, a buyer needs to remember they are dealing with another human being on the other end.** Most people are level-headed and want to do everything to move towards an easy and successful closing; however, there are sometimes folks who want to make everything difficult. During your contract, the other side can act irrationally. They can decide not to buy or sell for no logical reason. They can make unreasonable demands or threats. While it's in our nature to try to win every battle, typically fighting these people only makes everything worse.

2. **Regardless of market, price, or condition, a real estate market can go up or down and a buyer can lose money on a home.** There is nothing that states that real estate value always goes up. While everyone wants to make money when they purchase a home, a buyer needs to be prepared that making money typically is not a straight line of profits.

3. **Home inspectors and inspections are great systems; however, the most thorough and detailed ones cannot find everything wrong with a home.** With that having been said, a perfect home with zero maintenance does not exist. Therefore, the potential pitfall is that a buyer could move into a home that has a multitude of maintenance items that they did not realize existed. While it is impossible to know everything about a home, the job of the buyer is to do their due diligence to make sure they mitigate these potential problems as best as possible,

knowing that all homes have some issues. At the end of the day, a buyer just needs to know what they are getting themselves into.

4. **Issues with the title of the home, while infrequent, can also be a risk to purchasing a home.** The title of a home can be defined as the line of owners throughout the history of a property. If there were to be a "title claim" or a person who claimed they owned the home in the past but were never given credit, it could delay or even prevent a closing from happening. While these claims are few and far between, it is best to know about the possibility of them and purchase title insurance when possible. Good news is that any loan will require title insurance to be purchased by the seller or buyer before closing.

5. **Overall, there are risks associated with purchasing a home.** However, there are risks associated with basically everything in life. Some are avoidable entirely and some can be mitigated to a lower level. Statistics have shown us over the last 100 years, real estate is a very good investment so the reward, more than not, outweighs the risk. One of my favorite quotes is "Don't be fearful of risks. Understand them, then manage and minimize them to an acceptable level." Purchasing a home is no different.

See Also:
Chapter 1: What Does it Mean to Invest in Real Estate?
Chapter 18: What to Know During the Inspection Phase
Chapter 21: Common Move-In Issues

Chapter 12: How to Pick the Best Real Estate Agent for You

Like in any profession, there are some good real estate agents and some that are not so good. The best way to find out this information is for a buyer to interview a handful of real estate agents to find out which one is best for their situation.

1. **The best qualities to look for in a real estate agent are experience, trustworthiness, and great communication.** If a real estate agent has these qualities, even the worst transactions won't be nearly as bad. Basically, a buyer can alleviate the potential stress that could happen if they were to hit a speed bump.

2. **Experience is important.** An experienced agent has seen more than a less experienced agent and probably knows how to navigate more scenarios. Some transactions require some creative thinking, and an experienced agent may have some knowledge or even friends to lean on to make it less problematic.

3. **Being trustworthy is a key quality because a buyer should be able to fully trust their agent's advice.** If a buyer and a real estate agent are not on the same page, the easiest conversations and negotiations can be a problem. If a buyer doesn't trust their agent, that deal could fall apart entirely. A real estate agent might recommend a buyer accept a counteroffer with some interesting caveats, but if the buyer does not trust that advice, it may never go into contract. There will be situations where a buyer will need to put faith in their agent, and, if the trust isn't there, it will not go smoothly.

4. **Like any good relationship, good and open communication is key.** One of the best quotes is that "bad news isn't wine. It doesn't improve with age" and it is applicable within real estate. A good real estate agent will let their client know about bad news immediately so all parties can properly prepare. For example, let's say a closing is going to be delayed for a week. A good real estate

agent will let their clients know immediately so they can arrange adequate housing. Good communication can also apply to the agent-to-agent conversations. There are situations where agent to agent conversations can save a contract where the buyer and seller are at odds. Overall, if the agent is not a good communicator, stay away.

5. **Ask about fees for a real estate agent's services.** Most of the time, buyers do not pay their agent for their services; the sellers usually pay commissions. Typically, a seller will offer a commission to the seller's agent and, additionally, they will offer a cooperating commission to a buyer's agent to bring a buyer to the property. In most cases, this commission is a percentage of the sales price, but it could also be a flat fee. With that having been said, every commission is negotiable. Every market is also different. There are agents that charge more than market rate for their services and there are limited-service agents who charge significantly less. Like most any service in life, a client gets what they pay for. A more expensive seller's agent might cover all the marketing costs of the home whereas a less expensive agent may just put a sign in the yard and the listing online. These differences are incredibly important and should be discussed when interviewing real estate agents. Lastly, commissions are paid out at the closing of the property from the proceeds of the sale. This means that no commissions are paid up-front but are only paid when the sale officially occurs.

See Also:
Chapter 5: Real Estate Agents and How They Operate
Chapter 27: Working with a Real Estate Agent When Selling
　　　　　Your Home
Chapter 34: What Does Being a Real Estate Agent Involve?

Chapter 13: Kinds of Properties You Might Want to Consider

There are lots of options for types of properties available. This chapter covers most, but not all of them, and these are not exclusive categories (for example, a single-family home can be in foreclosure). In this book, we refer to properties as "homes" to be generally inclusive of houses, co-ops, and apartments. See what works for you.

1. **Single-family home.** A single-family home is the most common type of property a buyer will encounter. This is the standard home built on a lot that typically has a yard or some acreage. It does not have any "shared" amenities with any other properties and often does not have a homeowner's association (HOA) or governing body aside from the general city and state guideline. Typically, the owner of the property is responsible for all maintenance on this property, which is something that should be considered before purchasing.

2. **Condominium or co-operative condominium (co-op).** The second most common type of property is a condominium or co-op. Both are private residences in a multi-unit structure. In a condo, units are governed by a HOA. In a co-op, the apartment owner has an interest (shares) in the entire building and a contract that allows the owner to occupy the unit. Units are governed by a co-op board. While these properties don't typically have land associated with them, maintenance is typically managed through a monthly fee to the HOA or co-op board. In some scenarios, it covers all the exterior, interior common areas, and grounds maintenance. The owner is still responsible for most of the work inside the physical unit though. When considering a condo or co-op, it's important to factor in the monthly maintenance fee in addition to the cost of the mortgage, utilities, and other expenses.

3. **A property in foreclosure.** Foreclosure, by definition, is the action of taking possession of a property when the seller is unable to make the mortgage payments on it. Basically, the person or entity that loaned the owner the money takes the property and tries to sell it to recoup the amount loan. Therefore, when there is a property for sale and it says it's a foreclosure, this means it is being sold to make up for those funds that are not being paid back appropriately or timely. During a foreclosure transaction, a buyer is typically negotiating with a bank or lender who is selling the property. Note: this can mean that the closing could be delayed or tied up longer than a typical purchase. Banks move slower and often must get additional approvals before selling foreclosed on properties.

4. **A property in pre-foreclosure.** Pre-foreclosure is the first step in the foreclosure process, and it occurs when a lender or bank sends a notice of default. This notice states that a buyer is behind on their payments and lays out a schedule of how to get back on track. This typically occurs when an owner is 3 or more months late on their payment. Pre-foreclosures are often put on Zillow as a method to boost the number of listings they have available to share with the public, but a "pre-foreclosure" listing on the internet, does not mean the property is for sale. A buyer cannot view these properties and they are not available on the MLS. It just means the homeowner is late on their payments for whatever reason.

5. **New construction.** Everyone knows that new construction is a home that is being built brand new. The first important thing to know is that a buyer gives up a lot of their negotiating power when working with a new construction. This is especially relevant if the contract is written on a builder's contract rather than the official state purchase and sale agreement. A builder's contract will be weighted in favor of the seller and there will be less contingencies and legal ways to get out of it. Second, delays happen ALL the time. If a

builder's representative tells a buyer that the home will be done in June, expect it to be done 3 months later. This means that a buyer should be prepared to have alternative housing after the proposed closing date. Third, even though there may not be a traditional inspection contingency, it is still smart to get a home inspection before closing. Many buyers assume a new home does not have any issues and this could not be further from the truth. Builders are human just like us! Sometimes they forget to hook up pipes or drill holes where they are needed. It is just always smart to pay that extra money to protect the investment. Fourth, a buyer does have more customization options when it comes to a new construction, such as picking cabinets, paint colors, or finishes. Additionally, this is a good option for those who love brand new items. While the buyer might pay a slight premium for getting a totally new home, it will certainly have that "new home smell" that some buyers crave.

See Also:
Chapter 4: How do I Know it's Time to Purchase a Home?
Chapter 8: How to Find the Most Up-To-Date and Accurate Listings
Chapter 28: What are Foreclosures and Short Sales?

Chapter 14: Types of Home Loans

When it's time to buy a home, most purchasers need to obtain a loan. There are a handful of different loan packages that a buyer can, all with different requirements for each. Here are the different types of loans starting with the most common:

1. **Conventional Loan.** A conventional loan is a mortgage that is not backed by the government, and it is the most standard type of mortgage. A buyer will need to have a certain credit score (usually over about 640), have a specific debt-to-income ratio (usually under 36%), and will most likely need to put a minimum of 3.5% down as a down payment.

2. **Federal Housing Authority (FHA) Loan.** An FHA loan is a mortgage that is backed by the government and is, therefore, easier to qualify for. It typically requires a lower credit score and requires a minimum of 3.5% down as a down payment. One quirk with this type of loan is that the appraiser can demand that repairs be done as a prerequisite of closing.

3. **Department of Veterans Affairs (VA) Loan.** A VA loan is a mortgage that is backed by the government and is exclusively available to members of the armed forces. It is also easier to qualify for, relatively speaking, and the buyer can put down 0% as a down payment. This loan process also requires a similar appraiser as an FHA loan and that appraiser can demand that certain repairs are made.

4. **Portfolio Loan.** A portfolio loan is a mortgage package that will stay within the specific bank/company instead of being sold on the secondary mortgage market. In layman's terms, this loan is harder to qualify for and can have very specific requirements because the bank will be taking on the risk.

5. **Medical Professionals Loan.** This is a unique loan product exclusively available to persons working in the medical field. In this scenario, a bank or mortgage company is more willing to take on this type of debt because medical professionals will make more money down the road to pay it back. Interest rates, credit scores, and down payments all vary for this product.

6. **Down Payment Assistance Loan.** This type of loan is a program that varies from state to state and lender to lender. Typically, these loans are backed by the state government and are for lower income families. The qualifications are less strict than other loan products but some terms, like interest rate, are less desirable. To find out more information on these, talk to lenders and ask questions about their first-time homebuyer programs. Each lender will be different, which is why it's important to shop around as well. Your city, county, or state may also have first-time homebuyer programs.

7. **A word about Private Mortgage Insurance (PMI).** PMI a type of insurance that is often required for conventional mortgage loan borrowers. When you buy a home and make a down payment of less than 20% of the home's purchase price, PMI may become a part of your mortgage payment. It protects your lender if you stop making payments on your loan. PMI is generally not required when you own more that 20% of the home's equity. If you start with PMI and the market goes up, you may wish to get a re-appraisal; once you provide an appraisal that indicates you have more than 20% equity, you can likely get the PMI charges removed.

8. **Non-Conforming or Jumbo Loans.** These are large loans over a certain threshold that adjusts year by year. These loans are the riskiest loans a mortgage company or bank can do so the requirements to qualify are the strictest of all. You most

likely won't be using one of these for a first purchase in your real estate endeavors.

See Also:
Chapter 6: What is the Difference Between Banks and Mortgage Companies?
Chapter 7: How and When to Get Pre-Approved
Chapter 9: What are Closing Expenses and How do They Affect My Purchase?

Chapter 15: Location, Location, Location!

When it comes to buying (and selling) real estate, location is everything. It's not *kind of important*. It's not *sometimes relevant* in the process. Location is *everything* and all buyers need to understand this before ever starting the process of purchasing. What do you need to know about locations?

1. **What do we mean by location?** Location can include what state, county, city, or neighborhood the property is in (which affects taxes and resale value). Location can refer to many aspects of the property, including:
   a. Nearby green space and parks
   b. Nearby restaurants and retail
   c. Transit stations and commuting convenience
   d. Public school system
   e. Views and vistas
   f. Neighborhood walkability
   g. Community/neighborhood closeness
   h. Resale value (for retaining value)
   i. Investment value (such as in a fixer-upper)
   j. Location on street, such as cul-de-sac, corner lot/unit, or next to highway
2. **Most properties have some positive and some negative aspects to their location.** Each of these aspects affects the current and future value of a home. It can also affect your interests; for example, you may be very interested in school systems and less interested in transit options, or vice versa.
3. **How do you determine the best location for you?** It's a balance. You may want to maximize one aspect of location and minimize another that's less important. If you're focused on resale value, that could suggest different locations than needing a quick commute or tight-knit community.

4. You'll also need to find a location that fits in your budget. You can have it all- *if* you're willing to pay top dollar. There will probably be multiple locations that fit into a buyer's budget; however, of those locations, there will be a better or best location.

5. Ask your real estate agent their opinion regarding location and how to maximize what is important to you. Remember: they do this for a living and know the intricacies of specific cities and markets.

See Also:
Chapter 1: What Does it Mean to Invest in Real Estate?
Chapter 17: Negotiating from the Buyer's Perspective
Chapter 29: Marketing 101

Chapter 16: Showings!
Time to Go See Some Homes

Ahhhhh showings! This is widely known as the most fun part about real estate! A prospective buyer gets their time in a plethora of homes that could be the home of their dreams! In reality, it is more of a process than what gets broadcast to the world. Let's start out with the process and we will assume that the buyer is working with a real estate agent.

1. **Sometimes a buyer will send their real estate agent a list of homes they like and would like to tour.** These homes could have come from the buyer searching the internet or the agent sending the buyer a couple that might fit their needs. It is a best practice to prioritize your list and let your agent know which ones you are most interested in. If possible, pick the best homes that are near each other because that will be the best use of time.

2. **Real estate agents can also listen to what you want and make suggestions for properties to show you.** Once you have start seeing properties, a good real estate agent will take note of your likes and dislikes and keep an eye out for those types of properties. While it's best for the buyer to be constantly doing their own research, it is still helpful to have an agent who will suggest different areas and types of homes.

3. **Be aware there may be different types of showing restrictions on the property.** The easiest home to show is an empty home, which is often called a "go-and-show." A buyer and their agent can typically see this at any time of day for as long as they like. Most commonly, however, properties are shown by appointment. Typically, the seller is still living in the home and the agent must check on whether the seller can vacate the home during the showing time that was requested. Lastly, there are some properties that will not allow any showings.

They don't allow showings because there are tenants living in there or because the home is a tear down and is not safe. This occurs mostly with investment type properties but can happen anywhere.

4. **Although a buyer and their agent can try to prepare for every possible outcome of a showing, there are also plenty of weird things that can happen.** Sometimes a seller likes to stay at the home while the prospective buyers are there. Sometimes a seller is totally unaware that a showing is scheduled. Sometimes the keys provided to enter the home are not the correct keys. All in all, just remember to go with the flow. Do the right preparation and if it does not go perfectly, it's not the end of the world. Best case scenario is there might be a funny story about the first time a buyer was in the home of their dreams!

See Also:
Chapter 4: How Do I Know it's Time to Purchase a Home?
Chapter 8: How to Find the Most Up-To-Date and Accurate Listings
Chapter 21: Common Move-In Issues

Chapter 17: Negotiating From the Buyer's Perspective

Negotiations can be tense and contentious at times, but, if a buyer follows a couple different rules and tactics, they can come out winners every time.

1. **Know your negotiating power.** In some scenarios, buyers will have all the power. They will be able to make demands, determine timelines and price, and generally control how the contract process. Other times, a buyer will be at the complete whim of a seller. Negotiating power is mostly determined by the demand for the home. The best homes on the market for the best prices will have the most demand. A buyer might get the best home on the block but oftentimes they will have to work for it or must pay a premium in dollars or contract terms.

2. **Know what is open to negotiation.** Generally, everything is open to negotiation. You may want to negotiate for price, down payment amount, repairs (which you might not know about until the inspection,) time to move-in, time to move-out, whether appliances stay or go, or closing date in general. Note the seller does not control all aspects of the situation, such as the mortgage rates, but they can potentially negotiate on what is within their purview. Your real estate agent can advise you on what is negotiable.

3. **The most powerful tool a buyer has is their ability and threat of walking away.** No seller wants to have a deal fall through and must put the home back on the open market (unless they have another offer in hand). By drawing a line in the sand, buyers can often force a seller to accept their request even if it is not ideal for the sellers. The other side of this is that a buyer needs to be okay with the ramifications of walking away, which is that sometimes a seller will call their bluff.

4. **Both sides are working collectively towards a goal and it is not a good idea to be demanding the entire time.** If there is one thing (closing date, repairs, appliances) that matters a lot, a buyer should make it a deal breaker and stick to it. With that having been said, buyers with too many deal breakers can be seen as needy and unruly. Compromise is common and often necessary in a real estate negotiation from both the buyer's and seller's sides.

See Also:
Chapter 3: What is the Process for Buying a Home?
Chapter 11: Potential Pitfalls of Purchasing a Home
Chapter 19: When to Walk Away From a Contract

Chapter 18: What to Know During the Inspection Phase

Inspections are integral to the home-buying process. They provide critical information to the buyer about the state of the home. They can guide the buyer in the contract to request the seller make certain significant repairs. Inspections are also often the buyer's last line of defense to back out of a contract.

1. **Time is of the essence.** There are a handful of days, determined by the purchase and sale contract, to get inspections completed before negotiating a list of repairs to be completed by the seller. Keep in mind the seller may be unwilling to make any repairs; however, any repairs to be completed should be completed before the closing happens.

2. **The home inspection is a process and a document that helps a buyer make decisions; it is NOT a final say on every possible aspect of a home's construction and maintenance.** This is incredibly important to understand. While inspectors do their best to find any faults, it's impossible to be 100% sure about anything, and it's possible there are issues with the home that an inspector cannot see.

3. **Knowing that inspectors are human, it is important to compare reviews to find a good inspector.** While no inspector is perfect, there are certainly some inspectors who are better than others. This piece of knowledge could make or break a contract or save a buyer from closing on a home that has a bunch of issues. Remember, "buyer beware."

4. **Buyers, especially first-time buyers, should meet the home inspector at the home when the inspection is wrapping up to discuss the inspection.** This is important because an inspector will give their general opinion of the home and its flaws immediately. Inspection reports can be 50+ pages and be

incredibly daunting so having a professional break it down in person – even briefly – is a worthwhile endeavor.

5. **Be aware inspectors will find *lots* of issues, especially with older homes.** Issues with homes can include minor issues, like chipped paint, to major issues, such as outdated plumbing or wiring. It's easy to get overwhelmed with everything that is found in the report, but that doesn't mean you should abandon the purchase! Look for major or expensive issues, such as ensuring the foundation is solid; ensuring the home is correctly hooked up to the municipal sewer system, well, or septic tank; how much time before the roof needs to be repaired/replaced; the state of plumbing and wiring and whether the inspector recommends replacement; and whether the furnace, air conditioner, or water heaters are in good shape, etc. I (JW) tend to focus first on what are safety/habitability issues that would make it unsafe or impossible to live in the home (e.g., non-working plumbing, hole in roof), then other relatively minor issues (such as a non-working outlet, or replacing an older refrigerator), and finally personal preferences (repainting, remodeling).

6. **Consider what you want to request as contractual repairs.** Your real estate agent can guide you on what to request. Generally, it's best to stick to major and safety issues. Also consider whether you're willing to purchase the property anyway or walk away if the buyer doesn't agree to make these repairs. Be aware that you have some leverage: once you share the information with the seller about a problem with the home, the seller is obligated to share that information with any future purchasers. Sometimes the seller can just refuse to make any changes and wait for a buyer who will accept those terms; other times the seller is motivated to move the property and will pay for repairs.

7. **The seller can make repairs before closing or they can offer up concessions (most likely money) to the buyer, so they make the repairs themselves after closing.** Both situations have their

benefits. If the seller does the work before closing, a buyer moves into a home that does not require a lot of work upfront. The buyer will just have less work on their plate. On the other hand, the seller is going to fix the issues for as little money as possible. They may not use your favorite contractor or go with the most expensive bid. Remember to keep these in mind because they are negotiable.

8. **All in all, inspections are incredibly important tools.** For most transactions, don't waive an inspection. Also, remember that after this contingency is satisfied, a buyer is almost certainly locked in the contract.

See Also:
Chapter 14: Types of Home Loans
Chapter 25: Where to Start When Preparing to Sell a Home?
Chapter 28: What are Foreclosures and Short Sales?

Chapter 19: When to Walk Away From a Contract

One of the hardest things a buyer will do is walk away from the home and contract that they were once so confident in. They thought this home was "the one" but it ended up having some issues. Most likely these issues came up during the inspection phase but they also could arise during the appraisal or when dealing with the seller of the home.

1. **The most likely reason a buyer would want to walk away from a home is because of an inspection that reveals significant structural problems.** Several issues can come up while inspecting a home, but items related to the foundation and major home systems would be the most worrisome. Major home systems would be the roof, air conditioning, plumbing, or electrical. These big-ticket items are going to cost a lot of money and could potentially come up again, even if they are fixed. With all this having been said, I (ZB) have lost the most contracts over iffy foundations.

2. **Another reason that a buyer might want to back out of a contract is a bad appraisal.** Let's say the buyer is under contract for $300,000 and the appraisal comes back at $270,000. The bank is only going to loan the buyer enough money for a $270,000 purchase. Either the buyer is going to have to come up with enough money to bridge that gap or the seller is going to need to be willing to lower the price. Both outcomes would be tough pills to swallow for each side of the transaction. Sometimes it's just best to back out when there is a low appraisal.

3. **The rarest reason to back out of a contract is dealing with a hectic and unreasonable seller.** As we discussed earlier, sometimes a seller can have totally unrealistic expectations that make the entire process painful. These painful processes

can take a real toll on a buyer, and it may just be in the best interest of the buyer to back out using one of their contingencies.

See Also:
Chapter 3: What is the Process for Buying a Home?
Chapter 21: Common Move-In Issues
Chapter 24: Steps in Selling a Home

Chapter 20: Do's and Don'ts of Closing Week

Wow - It's almost time to close on the home! It's probably been a tedious process but hopefully, there was not too much stress involved. So as a buyer moves towards closing day, there are a handful of things that should be noted. Let's call them the DO's and DON'Ts of closing week.

1. **DON'T make any large purchases on credit during the last week of the contract.** Don't make any large purchases with credit during the entire contract. When a buyer makes big purchases during the contract that are not cash, it can throw off the debt-to-income ratio necessary to get final approval and close. The last thing a buyer wants is to hear from their lender that they can't get the loan less than 7 days from closing.

2. **DO get the cash to close ready the day before closing.** Whether a buyer is going to pay with cashier's check or wire transfer, make sure to handle this day before closing if possible. In today's real estate world, some closing attorneys won't accept cashier's checks. If the plan is to close on a Thursday, just plan to go to the bank on Wednesday afternoon. Every single person involved with the transaction will be thankful.

3. **DON'T make a stink of tiny issues during the final walkthrough.** More times than I (ZB) can count, a buyer has been upset that the air conditioning was left on at 75 or that there are a couple drywall holes. While there are specific issues a buyer should absolutely be concerned with, some small items buyers shouldn't dwell on right before closing. At the end of the day, there would only really be two options: threaten to not close and try to get the seller to fork over extra money, or not close and risk the seller suing. Do either of these sound like fun options right before making the biggest purchase in your life?

4. **DO respond to the lender in a timely fashion.** The lender will have deadlines that cannot be missed if a buyer wants to close on

the date that has been planned. A buyer must sign closing documents a couple days before closing to make sure everything is in order. If a buyer decides to put it off for no reason and waits an extra day to sign those documents, closing is required to be moved. Don't play with fire.

5. DO change over the utilities into the buyer's name and give the seller an extra day or two. For example, if the buyer is supposed to close on a Wednesday, tell the utility company to switch over service on the day after closing (Thursday). It is just nice for a buyer to give the seller an extra day to make sure everything goes smoothly.

6. DON'T bring friends and family to the final walkthrough. A buyer made a purchase based on their financial situation, their wants, and their needs. When friends or family are introduced before closing, they can easily make a buyer second guess their decision. While there would be no legal reason to back out, it just kills the vibes. Nobody likes vibe killers on closing day. There will be plenty of time to invite friends and family to celebrate.

7. DO bring friends and family to the closing table. This is one of the most exciting points of the transaction. Enjoy it and, most importantly, enjoy it with people that matter the most.

See Also:
Chapter 2: What is the Difference Between Buying and Renting?
Chapter 11: Potential Pitfalls of Purchasing a Home
Chapter 24: The Final Steps of Selling: To the Closing Table and
        Beyond

Part III. Settling Into Your New Home

You've just made one of the biggest purchases of your life and now it's time to settle into your new home. You have gone through a lot to make this happen and it's finally done! Remember: not everyone gets this opportunity in their life, so enjoy these moments! With that said, the work is never truly over when you own real estate. There are a handful of different problems that any homeowner should keep an eye out for.

Chapter 21: Common Move-In Issues

No home is perfect, and all homes require maintenance. In general, it's wise to prepare for the worst and hope for the best. What should you expect? Read on...

1. **What kinds of big-cost maintenance are needed?** There are several big system maintenance issues that need to be upgraded periodically:
   a. Roofs need to be replaced every 25-35 years assuming no weather or tree damage.
   b. Heating/air conditioning need to be replaced approximately every 10-20 years.
   c. Windows need to be replaced on an "as-needed" basis. There are 50-100 year old homes that still have original windows.
   d. Electric needs to be replaced or updated depending on city codes and if the home is ever renovated. Typically, if a full renovation occurs, updating the electrical system needs to be accounted for.
   e. Plumbing is like electrical. There are older homes that still have original plumbing, but if the owner ever decides to do a major renovation, it may need to be updated according to city codes.
   f. Appliances (refrigerator, washer/dryer, stove/oven, dishwasher, etc.) generally need to be replaced or repaired every 10 years.
   g. Flooring needs to be replaced on an "as-needed" basis.
   h. Painting/repairing home exterior needs to be addressed approximately every 10-20 years.
2. **Other maintenance issues require ongoing attention:**

a. Replacing light bulbs, smoke alarm batteries, and air conditioning/furnace filters.

b. Seasonal issues, like cleaning gutters, irrigation systems or weatherizing outdoor fixtures.

c. Pest inspection/treatment.

3. **There are also surprises,** such as leaks, termites, weather damage, falling trees, and animal infestations (birds, squirrels, rats, snakes, ants, mice) that will need to be managed.

4. **New homes generally have less maintenance than older homes,** because their heating/air conditioning, plumbing, electric, and roof are all new. While the major home systems (HVAC, plumbing, electrical, foundation, and roof) should be good to go, builders can also make mistakes. Sometimes the connections for these major home systems can be faulty or not hooked up correctly. A new build also has some general "settling," which means the foundation and walls can have some slight movement. The best news about this is that builders are often required to provide a new construction home warranty that covers a lot of these new issues. As a new homeowner, it's important to know what these warranties cover.

5. **Older homes have many years of wear and tear so common issues in the beginning may already be known.** Assuming the buyer got an inspection, it is smart to try to address any serious issues immediately. Plan to spend a little extra money addressing issues like leaks and older electrical problems. Windows in older homes are also a common location for issues. Since the home is older, a buyer may want to upgrade or retrofit the major home systems, so they are operating up to basic home standards. Set aside a couple thousand dollars just in case anything breaks within the first couple of months.

6. **Overall, a buyer should know that maintenance costs are expected.** While it is impossible to predict all of them, prepare

that they will exist. See the For Further Reading section for recommendations on typical repair/replace home maintenance issues. Save up some money before closing if possible, so that these costs do not catch you unprepared.

See Also:
Chapter 4: How Do I Know it's Time to Purchase a Home?
Chapter 13: Kinds of Properties You Might Want to Consider
Chapter 15: Location, Location, Location!

Chapter 22: Renovations:
Are They Worth It?

Renovations are something that every homeowner considers at some point. Rarely does a buyer get into the "perfect" home where they never want to make a change.

1. **Generally, homeowners should focus on renovating areas of the home that make them happy.** Most renovations are not going to make a property owner rich so focus on the items you want to change for your own wellbeing. If an owner just focuses on what is the "best investment," it may cause them to want to leave and sell sooner. Remember to make it a home before worrying about the return on investment.

2. **Are you planning to stay long term or to maximize your investment (or both)?** The struggle around renovations comes when everything is completed, and the homeowner wants to sell. How much did those renovations add to my property value? Does the pool make my home more desirable? Which part of my home should I renovate first? Consider when planning renovations what your goal is – most comfortable home, increase value, or a mix of both.

3. **What return on investment can a homeowner expect?** The place where an owner will get the most money back will be in the primary bedroom + suite or the kitchen, which will sometimes be recouping 50% of the investment or more. These are two areas where buyers focus on when picking out their homes. They can even look over flaws in other areas when the bedroom and kitchen are immaculate. For the next level of profitability, focus on the living space (i.e., living room or den) and adding additional square footage. You can expect to recoup about 25-50% of that initial investment in these areas. Lastly, focus on shared restrooms and outdoor living

space. These might not net the homeowner a bunch of money, but it will make the home stand out among others.

4. **Make yourself happy.** A homeowner rarely knows exactly what the market will look like when they decide to sell, but they do want to be the best home in their price point. These often-simple renovations can absolutely help with that.

See Also:
Chapter 1: What Does it Mean to Invest in Real Estate?
Chapter 14: Types of Home Loans
Chapter 24: Steps in Selling a Home

Chapter 23: Renting Out Your Home

A common practice in real estate is to buy investment properties and rent them to tenants. This is a great way to build passive income and have assets pay the investor residual income. There are multiple ways an owner can rent out their property and each of those ways comes with specific levels of risk.

1. **Long term renting** is one method of leasing property, and it is the lowest risk option. Long term renting occurs when a landlord has a renter in the property for 6 months or longer. When landlords decide to do this, they want the least amount of work and want consistent income based on rent per month calculations compared to short term renting, which is more volatile. In these scenarios, tenant turnover is typically low, which means the landlord has higher occupancy (and more consistent income.)

2. **Month-to-month renting** is another type of leasing that is possible. In this scenario, a tenant lives in a property with a lease that says they live there a month at a time until a mutually agreed-upon move out date. Typically, the rent is higher than a long-term lease, but lower than true short-term rental properties. This type is the least common because there is a lot of work involved to transition tenants and high levels of uncertainty. While landlords love making more money, a couple hundred dollars (on average) per month more than a long-term lease may not be worth the risk of uncertainty.

3. **Short term renting (such as AirBnb & VRBO)** is the newest type of property leasing. Short-term is a fluid term but it often means a tenant renting a property for less than a month at a time. Short term renting is a high-risk/high-reward proposition. In the best-case scenario, a landlord will have a high occupancy rate (70%+) and low costs. If these projections come to fruition, a landlord can make a massive amount of

income compared to their expenses. On the other side of the coin, a short-term rental can also be a money pit. Occupancy rates can be low, tenants can be dirty/loud/destructive, and local property laws can be prohibitive.

4. **Do your research.** Each market is different, and these risk profiles are not set in stone. They can fluctuate depending on your local municipality's rules, the time of year, or even with the political landscape. Do your research and then reap the benefits!

See Also:
Chapter 2: What is the Difference Between Buying and Renting?
Chapter 12: How to Pick the Best Real Estate Agent for You
Chapter 29: Marketing 101

Part IV. Selling Real Estate

So you have decided to sell your property. It could be time to cash out or it could be time to move for a job. It could be time to upsize because you are adding to your family, or it could be time to downsize because the kids finally went to college. It could be for a whole host of reasons, but the process remains largely the same. A seller should present their property in the best light, so they get qualified buyers to make the best offers that suit their needs. While not all sales are the same, following these steps will make for the most efficient and easy process.

Chapter 24: Steps in Selling a Home

There are lots of steps in selling a home. Here's an overview of the main parts of the process.

1. **What do you want?** - How much do you want for the property? What items to do you want to remain in the property? Fridge? Trampoline? Shed? Where are you going to move when the home sells? These are all things a seller should know when beginning the sales process.

2. **Find a real estate agent.** While this isn't required, more than 95% of homes are sold with real estate agents. It is a real estate agent's job to make sure this process is handled professionally and efficiently. Make sure to find an agent who has experience and that you know, like, and trust. It will make this process infinitely easier. Remember fees for real estate agents are most often paid by the seller.

3. **Prepare your home for photographs and then showings.** Professional photos are one of the most important things a seller can do to best market their property. iPhone photos are super tacky and do NOT put the home in the best light. Often, real estate agents will pay for these photos out of their marketing budget. Do not allow for a real estate agent to market your property without professional photos. Additionally, let the photographer do what they think is best when they are taking photos. They will often suggest moving items around your property: let them. They do this for a living so they know what will look best.

4. **Showing your property.** It is imperative that the seller leave the property during all showings. While it isn't always possible, it will be significantly more difficult to sell a home if the seller is at the home during every showing. Imagine if you had someone hovering over you when you were trying to make

an important purchase. This is what it feels like when a seller is home during a showing.

5. **Negotiate a contract that suits your needs.** This is the first phase of negotiations, and it would not be smart to agree to something that you are not okay with. Your real estate agent can help you with the contract; once the contract is signed, it is legally binding and incredibly difficult to get out of. A good rule of thumb is do not agree to something during the negotiations that you plan to try to get out of later.

6. **Inspection.** It is very important that the seller vacate the premises along with any pets during the inspection. Any time that a seller spends with a buyer's inspector could be deemed tampering with the inspector. Once the inspection is complete, the buyer will either accept the property as-is, provide the seller with a list of repairs they are requesting, or back out of the contract due to the inspection contingency. Note: there are buyers that will use this contingency to back out for other reasons. Don't get upset. It's typically not a legal battle worth fighting. Note: if the buyer lets you know that the inspection revealed significant damage, you may be required to disclose that to a future buyer, so it may be in your interest to address the issues now with a willing buyer.

7. **Lots of paperwork** - Since you have already purchased a home, this shouldn't be all that surprising. There will be a good amount of paperwork during the transaction. There will be paperwork that your real estate agent needs in addition to paperwork that the title company and attorney need. Review all the documents and ask questions when you have them. More than likely, all parties are happy to explain.

8. **Closing** – Closing day is often very similar for both buyers and sellers. First off, make sure the home is presentable for the final walkthrough, which often happens the day of or before closing. The general standard is "broom swept," which means floors are swept and all is tidy. Second, block off about an hour for closing even though it probably won't take that long as a

seller. Lastly, make sure that all items you don't bring to closing (extra keys, garage door openers, and appliance warranties) are on the countertop or in an easily accessible area in the home for the new buyer.

See Also:
Chapter 18: What to Know During the Inspection Phase
Chapter 30: How to Show Your Home
Chapter 32: The Final Steps of Selling: To the Closing Table and
         Beyond

Chapter 25: Where to Start When Preparing to Sell a Home

Selling a home takes a lot of work and preparation. It is incredibly important to get all details straightened out before starting to have buyers walk through the home. If the important details are not ironed out before going to market, any seller is going to have a more stressful situation on their hands that is easily avoidable.

1. **Step One: Declutter immediately.** This is one of the main reasons a home does not sell: it's cluttered and/or dirty. We live in a world where people accumulate items; clutter makes spaces appear way more crowded than they are. This can directly affect a buyer's mindset and push them to not offer on the property. The decluttering should be finished by the time photos are taken of the home.

2. **Figure out where you are going to live when your home sells.** This could be with a friend, at your parents' home, in a rental, or in the next home of your dreams. All these specific scenarios require different amounts of work and time management; however, the plans should be set out before the current home officially goes to market.

3. **What is the minimum you are willing to accept for the sale of your home?** Note: this is NOT the sales amount that will be listed but rather just your absolute bottom line. Why is this important? If this is an unrealistic number, the homeowner should not try to sell their home. It could be on the market for years! If it is a realistic number, then the seller should work with their real estate agent on best pricing strategies to get that amount and, hopefully, more!

4. **Touch up painting, fix any small issues around the home, upgrade the landscaping, and get the heating and air conditioning serviced.** Sellers want to present their home in the best light, know what is potentially wrong with the home,

MILLENNIALS' GUIDE TO REAL ESTATE

and limit their number of surprises that may come up. With that having been said, you don't need to fix EVERYTHING. Appearance should take priority over fixing small items.

See Also:

Chapter 22: Renovations: Are They Worth It?

Chapter 28: What are Foreclosures and Short Sales?

Chapter 31: Negotiating From the Seller's Perspective

Chapter 26: Potential Pitfalls When Selling a Home

Pitfalls for a seller are typically a little less scary than they are for a buyer. Since the homeowner has already gone through the process when they bought, it should be a little less intimidating. Additionally, the seller already owns the property and should make some money at the closing table. While this end should have less pitfalls, it does not mean they don't exist.

1. **Stale Listing.** What happens if a listing sits on the market for 6 months? 12 months? That is a very long time in most markets and can cause some serious stress for the homeowner. Frankly, there are only three reasons why a home does not sell: price, condition, or location. The homeowner should investigate lowering the price or updating the condition of the home to help it sell quicker.

2. **Lowball Offers.** What happens if a buyer offers a homeowner way less than list price? The short answer is "Nothing." There is nothing that states that a seller must respond to any offer they get. My recommendation would be to try not to get offended and to counter that buyer. I (ZB) have seen remarkable changes of heart that lead to clients going under contract after receiving a lowball offer.

3. **Bad Inspection.** What happens if an inspection comes back, and it says that the foundation is falling apart? Or that the entire HVAC system needs to be replaced? Well, it's not good news, but it's not the end of the world. In a typical contract, the seller can either have these items fixed before closing or they can allocate some money to the buyer. The buyer can also walk away from the contract assuming they have that contingency. These possibilities are totally normal! If the homeowner decides to make the repairs, make sure to use a reputable contractor, which leads me to the next point … Note that if the buyer lets you know

that the inspection revealed significant damage, you may be required to disclose that to a future buyer, so it may be in your interest to address the issues now with a willing buyer.

4. **Bad Repairs.** What happens if I complete repairs for a prospective buyer and then those repairs fall apart after closing? This part is important: USE REPUTABLE CONTRACTORS. If the homeowner decides to use an unlicensed handyman and something goes awry after closing, it could come back on them. They could be responsible to fix it again or they could get sued. Let's avoid lawsuits at all costs, okay?

5. **Title Issues.** What happens if the title attorney calls the homeowner a week before closing and says there are title issues? For example, Johnny inherited this home from his parents, but Johnny hasn't seen his estranged brother for 20 years. That brother might have a claim to part ownership of the home. While these horror stories don't happen frequently, they are possible. They are not fun, but most can be resolved within a matter of time. If the sellers have housing lined up, it could end up being a thorn in their side trying to get everything fixed.

6. **General advice regarding pitfalls.** Listen to your real estate agent during the entire process. A real estate agent will keep you in the loop about pitfalls and should warn you of them potentially happening. At the end of the day, life can throw some sticky situations your way and you may need to be flexible. Remember this is a business transaction and hopefully everyone is doing their job to the best of their ability.

See Also:
Chapter 16: Showings! Time to Go See Some Homes
Chapter 20: Do's and Don'ts of Closing Week
Chapter 30: How to Show Your Home

Chapter 27: Working with a Real Estate Agent When Selling Your Home

Real estate agents are everywhere these days. Most people who know one real estate agent end up knowing three or four. Why are real estate agents important when it comes to selling a home? What do real estate agents provide that make it easier to sell a home? The short answer is "a lot."

1. **Real estate agents are your representative in a complicated ecosystem of home-buying and -selling in the U.S.** Real estate agents have access to the MLS, or multiple listing service, which is the number one marketplace for homes that are for sale. In many cases, the MLS is the main feeder for internet sites such as Realtor.com, Trulia.com, and Zillow. If you want to sell your home, it makes sense to get your home listed in front of as many people as possible, and the MLS is the best opportunity to do so.

2. **Real estate agents do this for a living and network with other agents constantly.** That means the agent might have buyers that are looking for this exact type of property. The agent might also know of another agent who has buyers. If a notorious agent offers on a home they are listing, they could warn the client of the potential pitfalls before deciding. This all goes back to the famous quote, "it's about who you know, not about what you know."

3. **Real estate agents are negotiation experts.** Agents intimately understand the real estate market and what it will take to sell a home. When an agent understands their environment, they can advise their client to make the right decisions given the circumstances.

4. **Real estate agents remove stress and provide peace of mind.** It is their job to make sure all the deadlines are met, and all parties are informed throughout the transaction. If a buyer

decided not to use a real estate agent, all the logistical and legal issues would be entirely their responsibility. That's a lot!

See Also:
Chapter 12: How to Pick the Best Real Estate Agent for You
Chapter 29: Marketing 101
Chapter 34: What Does Being a Real Estate Agent Involve?

Chapter 28: What are Foreclosures and Short Sales?

The typical home sale occurs when a builder is selling a new construction or when a property owner is reselling their home or condo. When this occurs, the seller pays off any debts or loans at the closing table and takes the profit with them. But what happens when the seller doesn't make a profit? Or when the seller does not want to sell but cannot make their payments? These are called foreclosures and/or short sales. While they are similar in process, these two types of sale are not the same.

1. **Short sales are the sale of property when a seller takes less money than they owe for the property.** This entire process is flush with red tape and can take an extended time and effort. The real difference here is that the seller of the property, while not being able to make their payments, makes an agreement with the lender to sell the property instead of having the lender repossess the property.

2. **Foreclosures are a type of sale where the property's owner cannot make the payments and the lender takes the home back from the seller.** In this scenario, the seller either does not have the option to attempt a short sale or declines to do so. These types of sales are much more common in a down market, where something has negatively affected the job and/or real estate market. The last time foreclosures were a significant part of the market share was during the housing crisis in 2008 and 2009.

3. **Reminder: both short sales and foreclosures are often difficult situations for a seller.** If you are having to go through this, remember that it won't last forever and that times will get better. Additionally, while it can feel like the bank, lender, and new buyer are against you, they are often just doing their jobs.

No one wants to be in these situations so remember to be kind to all parties involved.

See Also:
Chapter 6: What is the Difference Between Banks and Mortgage Companies?
Chapter 24: Steps in Selling a Home
Chapter 26: Potential Pitfalls When Selling a Home

Chapter 29: Marketing 101

Marketing can be an enigma of trying to sell a home in today's market. Do I spend money? Where do I need to spend money? Should I advertise on Instagram, Facebook, or TikTok? Should I stage my property? Frankly, it's a lot more confusing than it needs to be. Here are some questions and answers that should help a seller see the light.

1. **Who should pay for marketing** This changes with every single client and transaction. Typically, a real estate agent will pay for listing photos on their own dime, but anything further is negotiable. Whatever a seller decides they would like to do, make sure to communicate it with the real estate agent. Some agents are willing to spend more to get the listing.

2. **What is the best marketing money can buy?** Professional photos. Hands down. It's not even close. These are the least expensive, lowest hanging fruit that exist, and professional photos help the most to sell the home. The goal when selling a home is to put the home in the best light, in front of as many prospective buyers as possible. Good photos will do this instantly. Professional photos are truly the gift that keeps giving. Lastly, if a seller interviews a real estate agent and they are not offering to get professional photos taken, it should be a serious red flag. Take heed.

3. **How much money should I spend?** Statistically speaking, putting a sign in the yard, and putting the home on the MLS with professional photos sells about 90% of homes. However, when a home is over $1 million dollars, it changes the calculus. When selling luxury homes, I (ZB) like to spend approximately 0.1% of the list price on marketing. For example, that would be a marketing budget of $1,000 for a million-dollar listing. It's a very rough number but it's an easy one to remember.

4. **Should I stage my home?** Staging means paying a company to put furniture in a home to give it the appearance of being lived in. Think of staging as having a home look like an interior decorator's dream for a brief amount of time. Staging is important where the listings would otherwise be totally empty. Statistics say that staged homes often get higher purchase price offers. I (ZB) also like to list my staged listings higher than a non-staged listing so that money spent is often recouped. While staging really is a case-by-case decision, the numbers don't lie. Buyers like staged homes better than non-staged homes. Typically, if your home is professionally staged, the seller is not living in the property. If a seller decides to stage a property with their own furniture, they can still live there.

See Also:
Chapter 8: How to Find the Most Up-To-Date and Accurate
      Listings
Chapter 30: How to Show Your Home
Chapter 36: Nine Keys to Success When Working in Real Estate

Chapter 30: How to Show Your Home

Showings are some of the most important moments of selling a home. It is the time when a prospective buyer is touring the home to see if they like it or not. A seller gets the chance to put their best foot forward with hopes that a buyer ends up making an offer. With that having been said, there are some golden rules with regards to what a seller should do during a showing.

1. **Vacate the home during the showing.** Leave. Do not sit in the kitchen. Do not sit in a car in the driveway. Leave. Go to a coffee shop or a dog park and give the buyer the chance to view the property by themselves. There is truly nothing more awkward in real estate than when a seller decides to remain in the property during a showing. In eight years in real estate, I (ZB) have never had a buyer purchase a home if the seller stayed while the showing occurred. It is very frequently a deal killer as the buyer cannot think about anything other than how awkward the situation is.

2. **Take all animals out of the home or, at a minimum, put them in crates in the garage.** A buyer's mind is going a million miles an hour during a showing, but pets take them out of the moment. Also, they could be scared or allergic to those animals. Pets just add another variable into the complicated equation of seeing a property.

3. **Fragrances can often be a turnoff to a prospective buyer.** Remember that entire goal of a showing is to appeal to as many buyers as possible and put the home in its best light. While the seller may love a specific smell, it could be horrific to a buyer. Again, the buyer will turn their attention to the smell rather than the different aspects of the home. If the seller does decide to have a fragrance, try to make it as "neutral" as possible.

4. Lastly, sellers should do a quick cleaning of the home right before leaving for the showing. It does not need to be a full, baseboard scrubbing, deep clean, but just a quick pass through the home to tidy things up. Not much is worse for a buyer's mindset than walking in a dirty home.

See Also:
Chapter 16: Showings! Time to Go See Some Homes
Chapter 18: What to Know During the Inspection Phase
Chapter 24: Steps in Selling a Home

Chapter 31: Negotiating From the Seller's Perspective

Negotiating as a seller is a little bit different than when negotiating as a buyer. If it is a seller's market, then they hold all the cards. They can ask for and negotiate almost anything into a contract. If it is a buyer's market, then it is a lot more like fishing and can be incredibly stressful. Either way, there are a couple tactics that every seller should know when responding to offers on their property.

1. **The first thing to know is that the seller has the most power negotiating position at the very beginning of the contract.** The buyer wants this home and, depending on the market, will jump through a lot of hoops to get it under contract. However, throughout the rest of the contract, the buyer will have a multitude of different avenues to either back out or to negotiate on repairs/price. As a seller, make sure to get the most out of the initial negotiation and ride the wave of satisfaction from there.

2. **Try to have the buyer remove or limit as many contingencies as possible.** A buyer with a conventional loan will typically have some type of financing, appraisal, and inspection contingency. Although that buyer would not be able to remove the financing and appraisal contingencies, they could modify the inspection. It might make sense for sellers to try to weaken the inspection contingency. A weaker inspection contingency might include a shorter inspection timeline or a stipulation that the inspection is pass/fail. Or clarify that the buyer may not request repairs because of inspection. At the end of the day, the seller wants the buyer to have fewer ways to back out of the contract.

3. **Once the inspection is completed, buyers are more likely to purchase.** The funds paid for the inspection are gone and,

frankly, buyers do not want to pay for a second inspection on another home. A seller can use this to their advantage during the typical repair negotiations. Does it make sense for a buyer to back out over a small item if they already committed $500? No! At the end of the day, a seller should try to use that knowledge to the best of their ability.

4. **Details matter.** Ask the agent who is paying for the title insurance. This is a small item that can save the seller a couple thousand dollars. Ask the agent if there is a way to make the earnest money non-refundable. This would guarantee that a buyer will close, or the seller gets compensated for the delay. Ask the agent if the buyers have submitted a pre-approval letter with their offer. If I (ZB) were selling, I would not accept any offer where the buyers had not spoken with a lender beforehand and have a pre-approval in progress. At the end of the day, purchase and sale agreements tend to protect buyers much more than sellers so it is integral that sellers do their due diligence on the front end.

See Also:
Chapter 17: Negotiating From the Buyer's Perspective
Chapter 22: Renovations: Are They Worth It?
Chapter 26: Potential Pitfalls When Selling a Home

Chapter 32: The Final Steps of Selling: To the Closing Table and Beyond

The seller is finally getting to the closing table. What should they expect? Do they need to clean their home before leaving? How quickly will they get their money? All of these are common questions during the last days before closing. Like many things in real estate, there are a handful of guidelines to live by to ensure a smooth transaction.

1. **Maintain the property and yard until the sale officially closes.** Just because there is going to be a new owner in a couple days, does not mean the seller gets a pass. This means mowing the lawn and keeping the home tidy. If only I (ZB) had a dollar for every time I had to pay someone to mow the lawn right before closing to keep a deal together, I would be wealthy. Please do not let the grass grow to knee height. In addition, the industry standard is keeping the home "broom swept" for closing so make sure the expectations meet that. "Broom swept" does NOT mean professionally cleaned.

2. **Help the buyer of the property by organizing the extra keys, extra garage door openers, and appliance/home warranties in one place.** My recommendation would be in one drawer in the kitchen. First off, the buyer is going to ask for these items. Second, it is just a nice thing to do for a new person moving into the home. Some sellers even like to provide a list of good referrals for renovations, lawn care, plumbing, etc. and it is always a nice touch.

3. **Set aside approximately 30 minutes to an hour for the closing to take place.** The seller's side of the closing is faster than the buyer's side, but it is nice to take in the refreshing victory of having sold a home. Most title companies will even provide cocktails if they are requested!

4. **Moving! When does it occur?** The seller should plan to move their personal items out of the property at least a week before closing. This allows for some buffer time to make sure everything goes smoothly AND for the buyer to do a final walkthrough without any furniture in the property.

5. **Lastly, unless both sides close in the morning, do not expect to see the funds from the transaction until the next day.** Remember the funds follow this flow for being released: buyer signs, lender receives documents, lender authorizes payment, buyer's title company receives payment, seller's title company receives payment, and then seller has access to funds. See why that might take a couple of hours? Trust the process!

See Also:
Chapter 19: When to Walk Away From a Contract
Chapter 24: Steps in Selling a Home
Chapter 27: Working with a Real Estate Agent to Sell Your Home

Part V. Being a Real Estate Agent

When I (ZB) was a year away from graduating from college, I had no idea where my career was heading. I ended up meeting with a local real estate agent during the holidays and it seemed like a perfect fit. Being a real estate agent is often considered one of the best fields to follow the "American Dream" because there's a low barrier of entry and your ceiling is as high as you want it to be. Given the right work ethic and training, you can go from nothing to something in a matter of years and build a career you never thought possible. It is certainly not easy, but I was always told that if I made it 3 years, I would be in it for a lifetime. After 9 years, I can now say it's worth exploring if it piques your interest. In the following pages, you will see what the job is like and what it takes to succeed.

Chapter 33: Should I Become a Real Estate Agent?

Being a real estate agent is a unique job. It has some of the highest highs and some of the lowest lows. It offers a nontraditional pay structure coupled with a nontraditional schedule. It's an incredibly fluid job that requires almost 24/7 attention and has a relatively high potential for getting sued. Is it worth it? Should I become an agent? Here are the pros and cons of the job and what it takes to navigate them.

1. **The pros of working as a real estate agent are plentiful.** Good agents get paid very well when they are successful. They have an incredibly flexible schedule where traveling and dealing with family's schedules is relatively easy. They get to be social butterflies so much so that it is part of their job. The only boss an agent has is themselves. They get access to some of the most beautiful homes in a particular city. It can absolutely be a glamorous job.

2. **The cons of being a real estate agent are also numerous and sometimes treacherous.** The stress levels can be incredibly high. The pay can be sporadic, or even nonexistent, if things are not going well. Clients call at all hours of the day and night. The job is 24/7, which includes holidays and vacations. Independent real estate agents also do not have benefits or a 401k unless they sign up for those items themselves. When transactions go sideways, real estate agents can be in the middle of potential expensive lawsuits. The lows can be very low.

3. **At the end of the day, it takes a certain type of person and personality to be a real estate agent.** They need to be self-aware, disciplined, and motivated. They also need to be relatively extroverted or can integrate themselves into communities where they can attract clients. They need to be

likeable and trustworthy. They need to be able to control their emotions to some extent. An extra bonus would be some handyman knowledge! Overall, a real estate agent needs to be a flexible, jack-of-all-trades that works well with people. Are you like that? Or can you become like that? Those are the questions you need to ask yourself.

See Also:

Chapter 5: Real Estate Agents and How They Operate
Chapter 12: How to Pick the Best Real Estate Agent for You
Chapter 36: Nine Keys to Success When Working in Real Estate

Chapter 34: What Does Being a
Real Estate Agent Involve?

Being a real estate agent is wildly different from how social media portrays it. From the outside, it looks like all real estate agents do is view beautiful homes and rake in money. It is much more busy work and errands than anyone ever sees. So, what does a day in the life of the real estate agent look like? Look no further.

1. **Mornings,** agents typically start off with emails. An agent will grab a cup of coffee and begin to follow up with clients, respond to questions, and generally make sure their contracts are in order. This means communicating with lenders, title companies, insurance agents, and inspectors depending on where in the process they are.

2. **As the morning progresses,** agents also look at Hot Sheets. Hot Sheets are the new listings that hit the market in the past 24 hours. While buyers have access to so much information on a regular basis, good agents are keeping their buyers informed with new listings they could have potentially missed.

3. **Lunchtime** typically means lunch meetings. Real estate agents are always trying to be in front of their clients, so lunch meetings are crucial. Typically, they are not discussing real estate the entire time, but rather just spending time and money on people who use and/or refer business to them to build relationships and trust.

4. **Afternoons** are often spent showing homes and consulting with clients. As the saying goes, "Work *on* the business in the morning so you can work *in* your business in the afternoon." The reason behind afternoon showings is that clients often need time to digest and decide if they want to see a new listing. Also, a seller might not be able to accommodate a showing request very quickly. Real estate agents do not fight traffic

often, but when they do, it is because of an afternoon showing during rush hours.

5. **Nights** are usually spent in meetings, writing offers, having long phone conversations with clients, and at networking happy hours. If a couple is making an offer, it is the time that they can be together on the phone. Does a first-time home buyer need help going through an entire purchase and sale agreement? This typically happens at night over the course of a thirty-minute phone call. Lastly, just like with coffee or breakfast meetings in the morning, real estate agents are found at happy hours frequently. They promise it's because of the clients and not because of the drinks.

See Also:
Chapter 16: Showings! Time to Go See Some Homes
Chapter 28: What are Foreclosures and Short Sales?
Chapter 33: Should I Become a Real Estate Agent?

Chapter 35: What is Required to Become a Real Estate Agent?

Real estate license requirements vary by state. Using Tennessee as an example, there are effectively 7 requirements that need to be met before the Tennessee Real Estate Commission will issue a license; these are generally similar for other states. See For Further Reading to review requirements for your state.

1. **Be at least 18 years old.** Easy enough!
2. **Be a state resident for at least 45 days prior to obtaining the license.** Not too hard!
3. **Be a high school graduate or hold a GED.** Important to know that any real estate agent applicants will need proof of this as well.
4. **Complete a basic principles course.** This requirement may vary by state; in Tennessee, it's a 60-hour Basic Principles of Real Estate Course. There are a variety of different ways that someone can complete this course including in person, online, on weekends, or even during nights. In Tennessee, this course will cost an attendee approximately $350 or more.
5. **Pass the state and national exams by scoring at least 70%.** These tests are administered almost every day of the week. Most states have an online portal to schedule these tests. An applicant can take these tests on the same day or on different days. Lastly, an applicant does not have to pass these tests the first time around. Check with your state for study materials and what happens if you do not pass the first time.
6. **There may be other requirements!** In Tennessee, newly licensed agents complete a 30-hour New Affiliate Course. This new affiliate course is almost exclusively offered as a take home or online class. It can be completed at any pace if it is the take home version.

7. **Within 6 months of passing the exam, pay a licensing fee, have a sponsoring broker sign the license application, and send proof of insurance.** In short, this means that the applicant needs to be hired by an office to work and pay for insurance. My advice would be to start interviews for offices after the 60-hour course or right after passing the exam. The insurance costs an agent around $200 every two years.

8. **Complete continuing education as required.** In Tennessee, it is required that agents get 18 hours of continuing education every 3 years. There is no retesting required.

See Also:
Chapter 2: What is the Difference Between Buying and Renting?
Chapter 24: Steps in Selling a Home
Chapter 29: Marketing 101

Chapter 36: Nine Keys to Success When Working in Real Estate

Contrary to popular belief, being a real estate agent is not easy. It takes a lot of hard work and perseverance. Being a managing broker, I (ZB) see very specific traits in agents who are succeeding. At the end of the day, it is up to those agents whether they follow through with these.

1. **Show up and be present in the office.** The most successful agents, even as their business is thriving, come into the office on a regular basis. I tell my new agents to make a routine to come into the office for 2-3 hours a day, even if they think they do not have anything to do. Even if most of the time is spent shopping on Amazon, other agents will see the dedication of showing up every day. It matters. A lot.

2. **Follow through.** If a new agent says they are going to call a client at a specific time, they better do it. If a new agent says they can meet at a specific place, they better be there. It is shocking to me how many agents think it's okay to blow certain meetings or showings off.

3. **If an agent in the office asks for help showing homes, jump at that opportunity.** An agent can watch a million training videos and classes, but nothing is as valuable as real-world experience. Additionally, if the experienced agent thinks the new agent did a great job, they will continue to call on them for help. Experienced agents are very protective of their business, but they also are desperate for someone to count on when they are in a bind.

4. **Have a client/contact database and update it frequently.** When I first started, my mentor told me to create a list of 50 people who I could call/email/text to discuss real estate. Frankly, that number is WAY too high. A new agent should pick 10 people who know, like, and trust them and take them

out to coffee or lunch. There does not have to be a set agenda but inevitably, real estate will come up. Once real estate comes up, just have an authentic conversation about your career. People want to see their friends and family succeed. Ask them if there is anyone they know who is looking to buy or sell real estate in the upcoming months.

5. **The new agent should find something they are passionate about and immerse themselves in it.** This can be church, the fan section of a soccer club, or a work-out group. Or it could be a networking group, a local volunteering spot, or a drinking club- it does not matter what the content is. What matters is that the new agent is authentic and commits themselves to being a part of it. A new agent should do these *because this is where your business will come from*. Clients like to use their friends or people with similar interests. In these groups, you will find both.

6. **Ask for help.** If a new agent does not understand something, ask questions. Every agent in the office was once new. If the new agent is not rude about it, the experienced one should be happy to help.

7. **Fully immerse yourself in real estate.** When a new agent says they want to do real estate, but don't quit their 9-5 job, it is a huge red flag. When I first started, I (ZB) had 2-3 night jobs at a time, but it meant I could make real estate my full time job during the day. Real estate will never take off for a new agent if they are only dipping their toe in the water. Clients take those types of agents less seriously. It is a huge leap of faith, but it will certainly pay off in the long run.

8. **Find a mentor.** While this piece of advice is not available to everyone, having a mentor could mean everything to a new licensee. This can potentially help them get clients and have someone more experienced to bounce questions and ideas from. When targeting someone to be a mentor, remember not to bother them about committing to mentoring. It needs to

be a symbiotic relationship. Let it happen organically if possible.

9. **Listen.** Real estate is all about listening and asking questions. Whenever I go to any meeting with a client, it is almost entirely filled with asking questions. The best real estate agents are also fantastic listeners; they ask one hundred questions, so they accurately know the situation and how to approach it.

See Also:

Chapter 1: What Does it Mean to Invest in Real Estate?
Chapter 27: Working with a Real Estate Agent When Selling Your Home
Chapter 33: Should I Become a Real Estate Agent?

Glossary

Active Listing: A property that is currently listed in the Multiple Listing Service that is available to see and offer on.

Affiliate Broker: A licensed real estate broker who is working as an agent and not operating his or her own office.

Amortization: The repayment of loan principal through payments of both principal and interest over a designated time period.

Appraisal: The act or process of developing an opinion of value for real property, which is often used in a real estate transaction.

Appreciation: The increase of value of a property over time.

Assessment: The assessed value of the property used to determine value for tax purposes. Property tax rate is applied to this number to determine the amount of taxes due.

Balloon Payment: The final payment of the balance due on a partially amortized loan.

Broker: a real estate agent who continues their education and successfully receives a state real estate broker license. Unlike real estate agents, brokers can work independently and start their own brokerage and hire other real estate agents.

Buyout: A sum of money used to exit a real estate agreement.

Capital Gains: A profit from the sale of property or an investment.

Cash Flow: The total amount of money being transferred into and out of a business.

Closing: The date/time at which a real estate transaction is finalized.

Closing Costs: The expenses over and above the property's price that buyers and sellers usually incur to complete a real estate transaction.

Commercial Real Estate: Any multifamily residential (apartment, condo, etc.), office, industrial, or retail property that can be purchased or sold.

Commission Splits: The percentage split between a company and a real estate agent that defines how much each party gets for a real estate closing. These are often negotiated on a year-to-year basis.

Condition: The physical state of repair of the building.

Contingency: A circumstance where an offer has been made and accepted, but before the deal is complete, some additional criteria must be met. Appraisal, financing, and inspection are common contingencies.

Depreciation: The loss of value of a property over time.

Due Diligence: The process of examining real property, or documents related to real property, over an agreed upon amount of time for the lender or buyer to reduce risk.

Electrical: All the wiring for the distribution of electricity, along with the fixtures and outlets.

Errors and Omissions Insurance: Insurance that a real estate agent must obtain before getting a real estate license. It renews every two years and covers mistakes that real estate agents may have.

Expired Listing: A listing that stayed on the market and did not sell. The agreement between the listing agent and the seller expired so it was removed from the MLS.

Finishes: The materials inside a property that are fixed in place. Common examples for finishes are cabinets, countertops, stairs, posts or columns, plumbing fixtures, and lighting.

Fixtures: Any physical property that is permanently attached to real property.

Flex Space: Space in real property that is flexible in terms of its use; e.g., an office that can be a bedroom or a workout space.

Flood Insurance: A type of property insurance that covers a dwelling for losses sustained by water damage specifically due to flooding caused by heavy or prolonged rain, melting snow, coastal storm surges, blocked storm drainage systems, or levee dam failure.

Foundation: The part of the building beneath the floor.

Home Inspection: An examination of a property's safety and current condition.

Homeowners Insurance: A form of property insurance that covers losses and damages to an individual's home and assets in the home.

HVAC (Heating, Ventilation, and Air Conditioning): The source of heating and cooling in a building, if applicable, and its distribution system.

Inventory: The supply of available active listings in each real estate market.

Kickout Clause: A purchase and sale clause that allows sellers to back out of a contract for a specific reason often related to the buyer's sale of their personal home.

Landlord: A person or business that leases a property to a tenant.

Lease: A legally binding document that explains the terms of a temporary real estate agreement.

Lessee: See tenant.

Lessor: See landlord.

Market Value: The value of the property determined by its market.

Multiple Listing Service: a database established by cooperating real estate brokers to provide data about properties for sale.

Office fee: The monthly or yearly fee charged by a real estate company for office use.

Private Mortgage Insurance (PMI): a type of insurance that is often required for conventional mortgage loan borrowers. When you buy a home and make a down payment of less than 20% of the home's purchase price, PMI may become a part of your mortgage payment. It protects your lender if you stop making payments on your loan.

Property Type: In residential real estate, it can be single-family, multi-family, condo, townhome, or zero lot line.

Purchase and Sale Agreement: A legally binding document that explains the terms where a buyer is purchasing real property from a seller.

Real Property: Property consisting of land and the buildings on it, along with its natural resources such as crops, minerals, or water.

Rent: The previously agreed upon amount of money paid from tenant to landlord over a period of time.

Repair Proposal: A proposal that marks the end of the inspection period and the beginning of the resolution period where a buyer proposes what repairs a seller might make. A seller can negotiate this proposal.

Sale of Home Contingency: A contingency that protects buyers because if an existing home doesn't sell, the buyer can back out of the contract without legal consequences.

Site-built: A property that is constructed entirely on your property board by board.

Square Feet: The unit used to measure the floor area of a space in a piece of property.

Temporary Occupancy Agreement: A short term lease that is executed as part of a residential sale.

Tenant: A person or business that occupies land or property owned by a landlord.

Title Insurance: A form of indemnity insurance that protects lenders and homebuyers from financial loss sustained from defects in a title to a property.

Withdrawn Listing: A listing on the MLS that was prematurely taken off the market before expiration for any number of reasons including needing repairs or lowering the price.

Zoning: A municipal or local laws or regulations that govern how real property can and cannot be used in certain geographic areas.

For Further Reading

Generally, real estate licensing is a state-specific industry. Requirements by state are often listed by searching for your state's "professional licensing requirements" or "real estate licensing" There are various online compilations that list requirements by each state, mostly by groups offering to sell training, available by searching "state real estate licensing requirements." Always check with your state's requirements before proceeding.

The following books can be helpful in your search for real estate.

The Referral Engine by John Jantsch (Portfolio, 2012)

The Power of Moments by Chip Heath & Dan Heath (Simon & Schuster, 2017)

Too Soon Old, Too Late Smart by Gordon Livingston (Da Capo Press, 2004)

One Mile Radius by Mark Deustchmann (Advantage, 2017)

Ninja Selling by Larry Kendall (Greenleaf Group Book Press, 2017)

Open For Business by Tyler Cauble (Lioncrest, 2018)

Make Your Bed by Admiral William H. McRaven (Grand Central Publishing, 2017)

The 5am Club by Robin Sharma (HarperCollins, 2018)

Mastering the Rockefeller Habits by Verne Harnish (Gazelles Inc., 2020)

The Culture Code by Daniel Coyle (Bantam Books, 2018)

Marketing Made Simple by Donald Miller (HarperCollins, 2020)

PTSD: Perseverance Through Severe Dysfunction by Reggie Ford (Ella Wenthom Books, 2021)

Acknowledgements

We wish to thank reviewers Gerry Vogel, Patricia Shea, Matt Feree, Bob Parks, John Shea, Caroline Melvin, Hannah Swanson, and Ragan Ogg. We greatly appreciate their perspective and insight.

About the Authors

Zachary Brickner is a Nashville native with 9 years of real estate experience. He specializes in the city's urban core, specifically Germantown, East Nashville, Sylvan Park, The Nations, and West End. He has significant experience working on sales teams and selling developments including townhomes, condos, apartment-to-condo transitions, mixed-use properties, and cottage communities. Zach is the former Nashville Junior Chamber of Commerce President, and was named to Nashville's *Top 30 Under 30* in 2018. In 2020, Zach was promoted to Managing Broker of his office. Since Zach became managing broker, his office of 55+ agents have produced two consecutive records years ending 2021 with $193M in volume and 450+ transactions.

Jennifer P. Wisdom, PhD MPH ABPP, is an author, consultant, speaker, psychologist, and principal of Wisdom Consulting. As a consultant, she helps curious, motivated, and mission-driven professionals to achieve their highest potential by identifying goals and then providing them with the roadmap and guidance to get there. Jennifer is the author and publisher of the *Millennials' Guides* series, including *Millennials 'Guide to Work, Millennials ' Guide to Management & Leadership, Millennials and Generation Z Guide to Voting, Generation Z's Quick Guide to Leaving Home,* and *Millennials 'Guide to Diversity, Equity & Inclusion.* She has purchased seven homes and sold five in Portland, Oregon; Washington, DC; and New York City.

Additional Books by the Authors

Millennials' Guide to Work
Jennifer P. Wisdom

Millennials' Guide to Management & Leadership
Jennifer P. Wisdom

Millennials' & Generation Z Guide to Voting
Jeremy Levine & Jennifer P. Wisdom

Millennials' Guide to the Construction Trades
Karl D. Hughes & Jennifer P. Wisdom

Millennials' Guide to Relationships
Kristina Hallett & Jennifer P. Wisdom

Millennials' Guide to Diversity, Equity, & Inclusion
Lisa D. Jenkins & Jennifer P. Wisdom

Millennials' Guide to Workplace Politics
Mira Brancu & Jennifer P. Wisdom

Generation Z's Quick Guide to Leaving Home
Denise Zorer, Diana Polus, & Jennifer P. Wisdom

Millennials' Quick Guide to Being a Boss
Jennifer P. Wisdom

Millennials' Guide to K-12 Education
Michele Gregoire Gill, Jennifer P. Wisdom

Millennials' Workbook for Diversity, Equity, & Inclusion
Lisa D. Jenkins & Jennifer P. Wisdom

Leaving Revolution:
How We Are Learning to Let Go and Move On
Jennifer P. Wisdom